HOW TO FIND

A JOB

AS A FELON

TABLE OF CONTENTS

INTRODUCTION

Finding a job is a second chance for many ex-felons who have decided to move on to a better life. Once they have served their sentences, don't you think it's time they are granted jobs? After all, employment is the easiest way to re-establish someone in the outside word.

Many ex-felons could have changed for the better if only they were given the opportunity to do so. Nevertheless, although the law protects ex-felons for fair treatment concerning job opportunities, jobs remain difficult to come by. The instability of our economy, coupled with the increasing competitiveness of other job seekers, makes matters worse. It's nobody's fault that jobs are hard to find. According to studies, about 80% of US companies background-check their applicants. And sadly, many ex-felons seeking jobs don't stand a chance against the average applicant.

Yes, jobs are necessary for the full rehabilitation of a person with a felony record. But realistically, is finding a job as an ex-felon even possible? Can people with previous undesirable records find jobs? How would you explain your past mistake?

Even if you are granted the same fair treatment as a regular job seeker, how can you prove to your potential employer that you are a better choice than the other job applicants? How can you prove you deserve to receive any of the jobs they offer?

The good news is, though jobs for felons are difficult to find, there are still opportunities out there. All you have to do is learn how to search for and find these jobs. Below are some suggestions that would help you find and land employment.

1.) Opportunities for jobs are usually found in professions that do not necessitate any background check. Online jobs, like freelance online writing, are possibly the best jobs for felons. Other good jobs for felons that do not require a background check are construction, food service, and delivery services.

2.) Look for possible opportunities from your local government. The local government and other agencies are happy to hire the services of people who have unattractive records.

3.) Go where your talents are. Common jobs for felons that involve using their God-given talents, such as painting, furniture making, arts and crafts and other occupations that harness the inherent creativity of the person, are good jobs for felons.

4.) Try real estate. Real estate is one of the best jobs for felons. Some employers may ask for felony records, but ordinarily, it doesn't matter. So, just be honest and focus on how you want to be successful.

5.) You can try to start a business. If you cannot find a job, you can start your own business. Why die trying to find a job where you work for a boss, when you can be the boss of yourself?

There are many ways you can find a job as a previous felons. Though it may not be easy and often disappointing at times, be strong and you will surely find the job that fits you perfectly!

Starting a New Life: Resume for Ex-Offenders and Felons

Despite the improving economy, ex-felons may still have a hard time finding employment. This may be attributed to the fact that there are a number of employers who are wary of hiring ex-offenders. Nonetheless, careful planning and re-aligning your job search will help you gain better results.

Here are some tips and career advice that can be used when drafting a resume for ex-offenders and felons:

Never conceal your conviction

No matter how tempting it may be, never leave off or hide the fact that you're an ex-felon. While hiding your felony record may seem beneficial, it may cause more problems and issues in the future. This is particularly true if your hiring manager discovers that you have served a prison term.

However, don't directly mention you have been imprisoned for XX number of years. This will give hiring managers a reason to discard your application. If your incarceration left a huge gap on your application, instead of directly stating that you have been in prison, use the functional format.

If a functional format cannot hide the gap, it should include a "will discuss during interview" caption. This will help you secure a chance to discuss and explain your situation, something you can't easily obtain when you directly state you have served time in prison.

View your prison term in a different light

Instead of brooding over your conviction, your application should highlight the skills and proficiencies you developed while incarcerated. For instance, if you attended crash courses in web site development, graphics design, and other computer courses, you can highlight them in your copy.

Again, a functional format is your best ally in this situation because it highlights skills and capabilities, instead of focusing on work timelines.

Seek assistance when writing

Unless you have a good hand when it comes to writing, it is best to seek assistance when writing your resume. A good writer can help you correct the flaws and minimize the imperfections in your document. Moreover, he can help highlight your expertise without focusing on your other issues, such as incarceration or your felony records.

Remember that a resume for ex-offenders and felons must focus on the applicant's proficiencies, not on his felony issues.

Search for companies that hire ex-felons

It is normal for employers to be wary of hiring an ex-offender. This may sound biased, but this is reality. In order to lessen your frustration and self-doubt, the best thing you can do is search for companies that hire ex-felons. This may sound difficult, since there are companies that claim to hire ex-felons even if they do not. As such, your company search should begin with your correctional or parole officer. Ask them if they can refer you to a company that welcomes ex-offenders. There are also numerous non-profit organizations that provide assistance to ex-felons who wish to rejoin the workforce.

There are many ways an ex-felon can enjoy better results from his or her job search. It may not be easy, since there are those who would discriminate against a former criminal, regardless of how he or she exerts effort to change his/her life. As a matter of fact, it may even be more difficult than serving a sentence in prison. However, it can be done. All it takes is a customized resume for ex-offenders and felons and the sheer determination to start over.

I'd like to offer a report on some top Jobs for Felons, lets's check through other chapters:

CHAPTER 1

Types of Jobs For Convicted Felons

SEARCHING FOR JOBS FOR CONVICTED FELONS

If you don't know where to look when searching for Jobs for felons, then you are in for a long hunt. These days, when an employer advertises a job that would be suitable for an ex felon, they get loads of applications from people who have no felonies on their record. It's no wonder jobs for felons are getting harder to find.

Combine this with a record of unemployment and you will soon become disheartened. All of that's about to change for you from this moment on. Read on to discover how you can land your dream job by the end of the day.

EASY TYPES OF JOBS FOR CONVICTED FELONS

When it comes to the different types of jobs for convicted felons, there is only one type of job that will hire you instantly without a background check. This employer does not care where in the country you live or what your previous qualifications are. They just want to hire you and pay you top dollar for your time and effort.

Who needs the stress of a conventional interview? It's no fun being asked very personal questions and being made to jump through the hoops like a trained circus poodle by someone who's probably half your age. Forget about all the other traditional types of jobs for convicted felons and say hello to your new bosses.

MARKET RESEARCH COMPANIES WANT YOU NOW

Market research companies constantly need information on consumer habits, and they pay web-based survey companies to conduct the surveys for them. This is where you enter the picture. These web-based survey companies will pay you approximately $30 -$40 per hour to fill in easy surveys on things like political views, what you think of a certain product, or even what you do in your spare time.

You and your email address remain confidential for the entire process, and you get paid at the end of the survey, so it could not be any easier. The best part is that there are hundreds of these survey companies on the internet, and if you join the right ones, you will make an absolute killing. Join the wrong ones and taking paid surveys will quickly leave a bad taste in your mouth.

Felons Can Make Money Online

How many times have you applied for a job, just to be rejected because of your felony? You need a way to make money without being penalized because of your record. You can earn money online, earning upwards of $500 per month doing little more than typing simple entries and answering simple questions. Jobs for convicted felons are practically impossible to find these days. But online, the possibilities are endless for felons.

What is this service?

This method of money-making online is called using "GPT" Sites or "Get Paid To" services. It's simple to make money using this method. So easy, in fact, the minimum age to join is 13 years old. A lizard could figure this out. Although using GPT Sites is easy, that doesn't mean it produces little money. You can make a few hundred a month doing this, while not working more than an hour a day (work more or less - your choice!).

How does it work?

To make money on a GPT Site, you need to find one where you want to sign up. You want a reputable, honest site that has been around for a long time. Then, you complete offers, do surveys, try free products, and more, all under this site.

They profit from your work and pass a percentage of the money onto you. For more information about a great GPT site that I use, click the link at the bottom of the page.

The offers usually take from 1 to 5 minutes to complete. The ones that pay the most money (for example, a free trial) might require a credit card, but don't worry. If you don't want to give out credit card info, you don't have to. There are plenty of offers that don't require them. Jobs for convicted felons like this don't come around often. Usually, there are few good things about a job - but read on to find out why you should try this!

Why are GPT sites beneficial for me?

Make a few hundred dollars per month.

Work as much or as little as you want.

Receive a check by mail every month consistently.

Free to sign up and costs nothing to make money.

Doesn't require a credit card.

Get to try free products, give your opinion, and get free samples - all while getting paid for it!

Jobs for convicted felons usually require background checks - none here!

CHAPTER 2

How to Succeed With a Felony

The reality of having a felony is that it is the equivalent of having the word 'untouchable' stamped large and red upon the forehead of the recipient. A felony is a suitcase of bricks that one must drag along beside them, in most cases, for the rest of their lives. It casts a dark shadow over integrity and credentials on job applications, rental applications, and even credit reports. This is the common reason most felons return to criminal behavior, feeling as though there is no other way. If one is willing to work hard, however, there is room for success.

Stay Patient, Stay Positive

It's easy to get depressed and lose hope after being denied even the lowest of jobs, the most rundown apartments, and being turned away by friends and family. The rebuilding process starts with restoring faith- faith in yourself and the faith and trust of others. Those who carry felonies will succeed in time at this first step by simply not going back to the behaviors that brought upon this unfortunate judgment. At times, this is easier said than done, but nothing comes without sacrifice.

Basic Survival Package

Success with a felony does not come quickly, so it is important to determine first what is absolutely necessary to survive.

1. **Find a Roof** Normally, the best case scenario is working out a deal with parents to stay with them in exchange for daily chores, zero tolerance for criminal behavior, intent to find a job, all the things that show motivation to turn your life around. It is absolutely critical that you do not burn this bridge, as it is the final net that catches you from hitting bottom.

2. **Find a Support System** It is imperative that the behaviors that led to the conviction of a felony stay in the past forever. Those days are over. To avoid falling back into your "old ways," you must have a support system, whether it be a probation officer, parents, or support meetings.

3. **Find Transportation as Required for Probation/Parole** You must comply with all the requirements that come with probation/parole, or you will find yourself sitting in prison. If you do not own a vehicle, I recommend reaching out to parents or those within your support system. If, for any reason, you are unable to find transportation, call your probation or parole agent as soon as possible to try to work something out.

Employment

Finding a job when you have a felony can be extremely difficult, so be prepared to be turned down for employment often. The key to finding employment as a felon is networking. There are a number of companies that will hire people with felonies; unfortunately, these companies rarely advertise this, so the only way to learn of these opportunities is by asking around. Probation/Parole officers are usually a good place to start networking, as they are in contact with felons daily and will be knowledgeable about the jobs that felons in the area have. Ask at support meetings; you may find someone who is self-employed and may be willing to offer you employment. Remember, at this point, any job opportunity is a blessing. Never turn down employment because it is "beneath you."

Staying on the Right Track

Once you find a job and start to save up money, life will start to fall in place, and things will become easier. It's important, however, that you never forget those who helped you get to this point, as you will have drawbacks, and there will come a time when you will, once again, need to depend on others for help. Continue strengthening your relationship with your parents. Keeping them involved in your life will reinforce their confidence in you. Keep going to support groups, offer advice and guidance to newcomers, keeping in mind that you were in their shoes once. Start developing a positive relationship with your probation/parole agent; their good faith in you can go a long way.

Finding Opportunity

As you continue to meet new people through work, support groups, etc., keep networking for better opportunities. There are always better jobs, better salaries, better benefits somewhere that can be found by talking to the right person. The important thing to keep in mind is that not all opportunities are advantageous, so it is necessary to research and weigh the pros and cons of leaving one job to go to another. If possible, take advantage of opportunities provided within the company you are currently working for. If not, do everything you can to keep a positive relationship with the company and make sure the job you are taking is a stable one, as a layoff when you have a felony can be a catastrophe.

Conclusion

Living with a felony is not easy, but fortunately, your past mistakes do not have to define your future. If you have a willingness to change and step away from a criminal lifestyle, then you will have a chance to take advantage of opportunities you never thought you could have. Start small, keep your eyes open, and use every day to prove to the world that your felony is a part of your past, not who you are.

Jobs For Felons - Is There Hope?

Finding a job can be a stressful and difficult process for most people. When you add a felony conviction to the mix, it becomes even more difficult. While the Internet is full of websites that offer false hope and promises for felons looking for work, there are also many valuable resources that can help felons find work, regardless of their history. It will take work, but those willing to put in the hours will have a better chance of success.

Jobs for Felons & Reentry Programs

The best time to start preparing for a job is while a person is still incarcerated. This isn't always possible, but job training in prison can benefit people when they are released. In addition, many states have re-entry programs that offer assistance to ex-felons as they try to reintegrate with society. This can be a difficult process, which is why so many people end up going back to jail or prison. The frustration of not being able to find a job because of a felony does not help the situation.

Jobs Training for Felons

After release, a person with a felony conviction may want to look into job training opportunities. In some cities, various state and federal programs have been set up to help ex-felons train for good paying jobs. This isn't always available, but it's a lead to pursue. If the government doesn't offer anything, an organization like Goodwill or one of many others may offer help with job training.

Seeking State/Federal Help

In addition to the many private and non-profit organizations that are working to help felons find work, there are many government agencies that may be able to offer assistance. The trick is knowing where to look for information and finding out who to talk to about your problems and getting help. If you don't ask for help, you're most likely not going to get any.

Never Give Up, Never Surrender

One of the most important things to remember for a felon looking for work is that they shouldn't give up or quit looking for a good job. The search can be difficult, but with persistence, it is possible to find a good paying job, even if you have a felony. Just beware of false hopes and promises offered by some websites. You should always remember there is a lot of work involved. If you do this, you're going to have a better chance of finding a job with a felony conviction in your past. Good luck!

CHAPTER 3

How to Find a Job As a Convicted Felon

Finding a job as a convicted felon can be a difficult task. In this economy, employers have the ability to pick and choose anyone they like, as hundreds of people are applying for the most basic job. A convicted felon has even fewer opportunities to get good paying jobs because employers insist on background checks.

So how does one find a job?

Finding a low paying job, like dishwashing, line cook, laundry, or gardening, doesn't usually require a background check, and one could find these jobs by looking online at Yahoo Jobs for example.

The question should be, how does one find a good paying job?

You CREATE one! Have you ever thought of owning your own business? Not working for minimum wage, getting a fresh start, or never going back in debt. There are communities of people making money online, and they help each other because, when one succeeds, they all succeed. There are no background checks. Wveryone is the same. We all support each other, and nobody will ever know they are giving money to you. Yes, I said giving money - this is a completely legitimate career where you can make unlimited amounts of money promoting other people's products.

Has anybody ever helped you succeed?

Within these business communities, everyone helps each other, and we learn from each other. Whether you are making $100,000 a month or $10 month, whether you are a firefighter or a convicted felon, whether you have experience or not, it doesn't matter - the materials, people, and tutorials are tried and tested to make you succeed. You don't have to be embarrassed asking questions or getting help. We are here for you, and you are here for us. It's that simple.

How much does it cost?

I found one community last year after not being able to find a job that could pay the bills. I had little extra money to spend to start a business but wasted $400 on a different affiliate training programs with no support or community base to help when I had questions (which was almost immediately). When you look to buy a program to get your internet business started, look to see if there are forums, free webhosting, free support, free on-going training, and that training is in print and video. You should also look to see if they have the following:

- ❖ *Personal blogs*
- ❖ *Organization tools*
- ❖ *More than a few thousand members*
- ❖ *Owner participation in the success of the members*
- ❖ *Web Page template for your website*
- ❖ *Jobs for writing, developing, blogging, etc.*
- ❖ *How long does it take to make money?*

It depends on your effort. You will not make money if you sit there and do nothing. You have to go through the tutorials and learn about affiliate marketing. I made my first dollar about two weeks after signing up.

Good Luck and Don't Quit!

CHAPTER 4

Felon Job Resume - Tips for Quality Resumes for Felons

Resume tips for felons are a huge help. It is a good way to rehabilitate someone by helping him or her to find a job from which he can start over. New jobs can help ex-felons become a part of society. Jobs are more than just therapy to the ex-felons. Finding a job is the best way they can reintroduce themselves to the community in which they live, and everyone needs help with resumes for felon jobs.

Creating a resume is something many job seekers find difficult to do. Even more difficult is if you need to create a resume for an ex felon. Should you keep the bad record a secret? How will you mention the felony?

Resumes are created to highlight the best side of a person. However, they need to be honest and accurate. So, how are you going to do this? Good resume help for felons should be able to balance the positive and the negative side of a person.

Below is a good list of resume tips to help felons who are willing to start over by finding a good job.

Focus on the Qualifications:

An ordinary resume usually highlights the employment record of a person. Highlighting the previous employment record will show the responsibilities that a person previously held and how long they maintained a job. However, since the person is in prison, there is a huge gap of years when he was unemployed from his previous employment to the present date. So, instead of focusing on their previous employment, you can highlight their qualifications.

You may write the resume the way you write a new grad's resume. You may cite the educational attainment, other qualifications like special seminars, workshops, and special trainings attended. If they are a professional, include the licenses. Then you can place the employment history at the bottom.

Mention the Felony in the Interview, Not on the Resume:

Ordinarily, you choose which experience to write on your resume. If you, for instance, worked in a company and was fired after a month, it would be wise not to mention it in your resume. What about the felony? Should you mention your conviction?

The answer is "NO." No, you do not have to mention it. Though there might be a break in the years of your employment history, it is better to mention your felony in the interview.

Yes, you are worried about honesty. The thing is, you do not have to lie. Supposed you were incarcerated for 5 years from 2004-2009. The following example will show you how you can deal with the dates you have spent in jail.

EMPLOYMENT HISTORY:

• Self Employed: September 2019 - Present

• Unemployed [to be discussed in the interview]: 2014-2019

Notice the dates on 2014 to the year 2019? It says "Unemployed [to be discussed in the interview]: 2004-2009." This is a way you can consider your felony charges without mentioning it on paper.

An interviewer will surely ask why you were unemployed during those times. Honestly come clean about your felony charges then tell the interviewer that you want to start anew. Focus your answer on starting over and trying to follow the law this time. Then you can bring the conversation to your qualifications and why you should be hired.

Create a Cover Letter:

Again, avoid mentioning that you are an ex-felon. You need to explain in brief paragraphs about your qualification and why the company needs you. Write the letter the way you would write an ordinary cover letter. Tell, but not expound, that you have made some mistakes in your past, and whatever they are, you are willing to change for the good. Add an explanation of how proud you are to be on your current path and how you would like to better yourself. Then ask for an interview to explain your unique situation.

If you are an ex-felon, you may not be able to correct and undo your former mistakes, but you can still do many things to make your future a little brighter. We all go through difficult times, but what is important is that we are able to stand from whatever problems we encountered.

Hopefully, the tips we provided will help you deal with your unique circumstance. Surely, resume help for felons is difficult to find. But remember, there is nothing in this life that comes to us easily. Persevere, and with the help of these resume tips for felons, you'll be able to create a successful resume.

Top 9 Job Tips - Employment For Convicted Felons - Easy Tips to Get You Earning Money!

Any convicted felon knows how hard it is to find a job. Let's be honest; employment for convicted felons isn't top priority to an employer. These tips will help you earn money as well as find a job.

Top 9 List

#9 - Be honest; don't lie about your convictions. If your employer does a background check later, you will almost definitely be fired.

#8 - Many employers will ask the question "How would others describe you?" or something similar. Be ready for this and don't use answers like: "I'm nice, hard working." Be unique and use an answer like: "I am a team player and can cooperate effectively. I'm efficient in a multi-tasking environment, and I am a reliable, honest employee."

#7 - If an employer asks about your felonies, make it clear that you made a mistake, and it has no bearing on your effectiveness or your work ethic. Focus on what you've learned from that experience.

#6 - When filling out application forms, use good handwriting and take your time. Especially if the manager reads the applications, good handwriting is their first impression of you. If you are sloppy or have many mistakes or grammar errors, they will judge you, and it could cost you the job.

#5 - Dress appropriately for your interview. You have enough obstacles as a felon, so you need to look as sharp as you can. Get a haircut and don't wear sneakers. Find a cheap, nice looking pair of dress shoes at Payless - even Walmart.

#4 - Try to network with other people; they may be able to find you a job. If possible, try to get in with a family business. They will be happy to hire you while you look for a more permanent job.

#3 - Do volunteer work around the community. This looks good on your resume and shows that, just because you have a criminal record, it doesn't mean you are a bad person. Employment for convicted felons is easy when you show you care.

#2 - Ask to speak with the manager after you fill out your application. Be the first to offer a firm handshake, look them in the eyes, and greet them. Tell them you applied for the position and that you hope to hear from them.

#1 - Consider starting a business and employ yourself. Many successful felons have made a career this way. If you can, try to start a side business while looking for a job. Employment for convicted felons is scarce, so consider being your own boss.

CHAPTER 5

Tips for Finding the Best Jobs for Felons

Finding jobs for felons has been too difficult for far too long. High-paying jobs for felons are especially hard to find in today's tough economic times, but tough doesn't mean impossible. If you've had trouble finding jobs for felons that pay well, read on!

A good tip is to look for employment for felons that either requires no background check or is open to people with a past. It also has to be a position that you are qualified for; otherwise, you will be setting yourself up for failure. It's a good time saving idea to apply only to companies where you'd otherwise be qualified and a good fit.

Tips to find companies that hire felons:

1. First, you have to evaluate yourself. Are you a good candidate for the career you want? Do you have the training and skills needed? Do you have any experience? Do you have any character references to show you have rehabilitated yourself?

2. Second, companies that hire felons don't fall out of the sky. You have to actively look for them. Use your networking skills to find a good job. Call and ask your friends, family, fellow church members, former co-workers, etc. for help looking for a job.

3. Then you might want to upgrade your skills, especially if you have not had any recent training or work history. Not all jobs for felons require training, but this will make you more attractive to potential employers. Hopefully, if you can get training, then you can advance your career and earn more.

4. It's helpful to check government or non-profit organizations that can help you in your search for a job. Ask your local or state employment agency if there are any resources for felons in your location. In some states, there are even job fairs for offenders, where there are hundreds of companies that hire felons.

5. Last, employment for felons is available, but to get hired, you have to know how to play the game. Jobs for felons are very competitive, and if you don't know how to present yourself properly, then you will lose out. When you start looking for jobs that hire felons, you should take steps to learn how to create a good resume, dress for a job interview, answer difficult interview questions, and present yourself as a good candidate for the job.

There is a problem finding jobs that hire felons, but there are many jobs for felons available, such temp work, truck driving, construction work, food service job like waiters, counter attendants, bus staff, etc. The problem with some of these felon friendly jobs is that many people feel they don't pay well or do not allow for career advancement.

Sometimes, this can be the cause for ex-offenders turning to crime again if the ex-offender feels he is stuck with only low-paying job for felons and can't improve himself.

However, although ex-convicts who have just gotten out of prison or don't have marketable skills may find low-paying jobs at first, they are still quite valuable.

Why are even low-paying jobs for felons good? Consider these three things:

• It's easier to get a job if you already have a job. You will have money to fund your search for higher-paying felon friendly jobs. Also, having new co-workers means you will expand your social network of people who may be able to help you find a good job.

• You can use these low-paying jobs for felons to build a work history – it's better than having a long period of unemployment on your resume.

• The longer you are gainfully employed, the less relevant your felony record will be the next time you look for high-income companies that hire felons. What seems like an insurmountable barrier when you are fresh out of prison will not be as difficult to overcome once you have a few years of work history.

The truth is, when it comes to jobs for felons, unless you are lucky, you will probably have to work your way up from the bottom.

On the other hand, there are some job opportunities for felons that are high-paying. We have some examples and directions to jobs for convicted felons that are exciting and pay well but don't require background checks.

Tips to Help Convicted Felons Get Jobs

Getting a job with a felony is no easy task. I know from personal experience. There are many techniques to better your chances of getting hired at a job as a convicted felon, so I compiled this list of 10 tips to help you start working with a felony conviction:

1. Make a list of possible jobs: There are many jobs that a felony will automatically bar you from getting, i.e., banks, police force, hospitals/nursing home, depending on the state regulations. Think logically about the chances of you getting hired dependent on your conviction.

2. Fill out applications: Start filling out tons of applications at the places from your list. A wise man once told me, if you are looking for a job working 8 hours a day, you should be putting in 8 hours a day finding a job. This holds even more value for felons, seeing as it is much harder to get a job with a felony.

3. Be honest: When filling out an application, always be honest and put your felony down where it asks. If you get hired and later they find out about it, chances are you will be fired. I suggest also writing, "I will discuss upon interview."

4. Be prepared with a good explanation: Prepare a good statement about what happened and how you have changed yourself/fixed the problems you had. If you have a good statement prepared, then you can hopefully find an employer who will be sympathetic to your situation.

5. Dress nice: Show that you really want the job. Sometimes, it feels silly dressing up for an interview, but going that extra mile proves you want it! Employers notice these things.

6. Go back to school: You can always enroll in school and further your knowledge for a specific job. Going back to school will help you because you will be better equipped for a good job, and it shows that you have grown out of your ways. School is a good way to show responsibility.

7. Join the army: The Army is a good place to get a new start for felons. There are many benefits to joining the Army, such as college, discipline, and real-world experience. Think about the pros and cons before joining the Army.

8. Try to seal your offense: Talk to your attorney or probation officer to find out what the stipulations are for getting your felony removed.

9. Start small: You will have to start small and work your way up. Having a felony means you need to put in the extra work. Prove yourself and get a better position at a job you land. Stay determined!

10. Make your own business: Probably the best option is to become self-employed. There are many ways to start making money as a felon online.

I hope this E-book has helped and will continue to help you on your job hunt and get you back to work, successfully employed!

Thank you again for downloading this book!

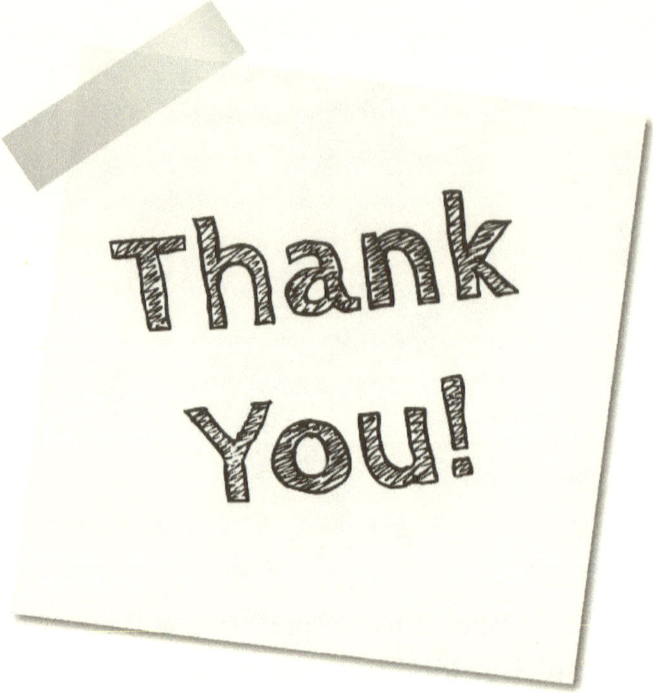
Thank
You!

.

www.ingramcontent.com/pod-product-compliance
Lightning Source LLC
Chambersburg PA
CBHW020332290526
45785CB00007B/3030